To Joy,

with all best wishes,

Martin & Jane

28. July. 2019

Song of France

To our friends in the Haute-Loire.

With thanks to Alan Afif for reviewing an early draft and to
Janet Ardavan for detailed comments.

First published in Great Britain 2019

Text copyright © Martin Evans
Illustrations © Jane Evans

The moral right of the author has been asserted.

Stamford Press
3–4 Wellington Lane
Stamford PE9 1QB

ISBN 978-0-955-36791-5

Printed in the UK by Biddles

Song of France
Ode to the Haute-Loire

Martin Evans

Illustrations by Jane Evans

1

We've been crossing over on the sea,
sometimes under it as well,
driving down the long way here,
always twice, sometimes thrice,
for well on thirty year.

From the north, you climb up into the valley
between Ollières and Achon
(*sucs* they call these rocky domes, made of stone that sings
if handled with a hammer and cleaved as thin as wings
to cover people's homes),
passing on the roadside gold letters on grey face,
that tell of two young local men war-murdered at this place
—for being patriots, that's why—
then round the bend, La Testavoyre, scratching at the sky.

From the south, you come down into the valley
where the turtle rock looks out
over waves of cloud-swept pastures rolling all about,
and marvel at three *sucs* lined together in a row
that cross the fells and wooded swells of ancient lava flow.
Each time I take it in anew, it always looks as good,
better than I thought I knew or hoped it really would.

Welcome to our valley of the Auze; it isn't very far
before it joins the Lignon and they together meet the Loire.

2

When I was eight with years to gain, soon after war had gone,
for holiday we took the train to Chambon on the Lignon,
sometime, somewhere, we made a stop, after crossing France at night,
lying luggage-like on rack atop I woke to morning light,
through hissing steam came platform cry *café au lait et croissants!*
that got me up with open eye to fill my breakfast want.

Then to my great aunt's house among the scented pine,
standing high up in the woods above the railway line,
on the terrace in the sun we drank from two-eared bowls,
smeared black honey on our bread, munched raisin-studded rolls,
then I'd go running down the hill when La Micheline came by;
I can hear its Eeyore siren still and its long-departed sigh.

One hot day 'neath blue sky calm, we set off across the land,
up stony tracks to mountain farm with walking sticks in hand,
my father swapped his chocolate bar for a lump of goaty cheese,
then on we climbed up high and far through woods of spiky trees,
like a mountain goat my mother said as with nimble jump and hop,
I bounded up the slope ahead to stand on Lisieux's top.

Sat by our door, now old and grey, I can see this legendary peak,
from sixty-seven years away I can hear my parents speak,
and though my roots can't reach as far as those grown from this place,
perhaps my tender footprints here give me some claim to space.

As time has passed—I don't know how—we've come to know so many,
of those who live around here now, our friends extraordinary;
we have watched them marry, children beget, and missed them when they'd gone,
just memory now when we first met and they kindly took us on.

3

But our first encounter with new neighbour did not augur well,
what it meant now we know, but then we couldn't tell.

One February day in biting wind, the light about to go,
we crunched across a frosty field to figures crouching low,
a bloody knife we saw one wield, the other pulled at guts,
plunging entrails in a brook, engrossed as we came up,
but this was not for us to stand and look, not our concern this private deed;
it's us who've bought that house, we said,
but nosy us they didn't need: a muttered nod, few words to share,
water running red.

We waited awhile but no more came, they wanted to be alone,
so back we went in sinking dark, feeling frozen to the bone.

It was later that we came to hear the custom of the land:
the pigs are killed at start of year to make sausages by hand;
for these Auvergne is lauded, especially Haute-Loire,
hung up to cure they're hoarded, much sought for from afar.

And of course we have to say we quickly came to find
Arsène Lechaine we'd met that day would be a neighbour kind:
many mornings we'd come down to find *légumes* by the door,
usually lettuce fresh from ground; another week there'd be some more.
And every year we would be favoured with some sausage he had made;
to me it seemed much better flavoured than that for which we paid.

4

He'd inherited his brother's house just up the road next door,
behind a muddy farmyard as most had lived before,
within a palisade of timber stacked around like castle walls,
to keep him warm in winter and safe from deep snow falls.
One room below, the hay above, the precious cows close kept
in a manger he could see from the corner where he slept.

Arsène had never married and now lived there quite alone,
his weakly sister having gone to be cared for in a home.
He'd spent his whole life working on other farmers' lands,
his clothes were old and torn, there was dirt upon his hands.
Though clogs were often on his feet, he never looked the least forlorn,
as he walked his cows back up the track to bed them down 'til dawn.

It was all he knew about what to do with his long retired days,
he owned the time—that was his due—but he couldn't change his ways.

5

Until two years before we came, Arsène and sister Adrienne
had been living just the same (many years from way back when)
in the house now ours to call. From hill itself it seems it grows:
basalt blocks for strongest wall, grey armoured roof of *lauzes*
(made from the special stone that sings
if handled with a hammer and cleaved as thin as wings).

A standpipe at the door beside served all their needs it seems,
much better than the well outside—one tap supplied their dreams;
but for us, of course, it did behove to put in baths and showers,
flushing toilets, electric stove, by the door to set out flowers.

What our neighbour made of all this, as the workman came and went,
we never knew but took a guess: too much money quickly spent?

6

So now we had a second home, but should we feel some guilt?
at least we'd brought it back to life, kept it looking as was built.

We did have plans to 'do up' the barn, a cathedral of wormed beams,
but the chance to buy another house put paid to those loose dreams.
We let Arsène stand his tractor there on the dusty first floor planks,
and later plastic bags of bags of hay and did not seek his thanks.

It puzzled him we'd no real use for this hall of wood and stone,
hard to explain we chose this place for love of barn alone.

We've treated it for woodworm, shored up its leaning walls,
the leaking roof's now dry and firm, we've kept the cattle stalls,
but there remains so much to do and we cannot face the task –
we have at least made sure it's sound and if anyone should ask
the answer is we chose to spend tight money on 'the other end.'

This 'other end' was a separate house attached to our barn wall,
always empty since we'd been here, hardly ever used at all.
It seems its owner only came for a day or two a year,
had a picnic in the garden and again would disappear.

When we ourselves appeared again after time in England spent,
it seems everyone was keen to know what would be our intent.

Good Monette came rushing round to make sure we'd heard the news,
like many of our nearby neighbours she didn't want for us to lose.
With second house now up for sale, it was a unique chance
for us to enjoy the full extent of this property in France.

However, there was one major snag, for we needed the field in front;
if we were going to spend so much, we couldn't risk it on a punt
and trust to luck it would legally stay land strictly for non-build,
or else one day we could discover with new houses it was filled.

Even though the house and the field belonged to one family,
the agent firmly told us for sale the field would never be.
He did his very professional best to create a sense of strong demand
by bringing as many people to view as he was able to command.
There were indeed a few who came to take a look around;
we talked to one who stayed outside wearing a puzzled frown:
why I'm here I've no idea—I'd asked for a flat in town!

Most asked about the iconic barn, were sorry it wasn't for sale,
which made us realize all the more we didn't want our bid to fail
for then we'd have the building whole (chances like this were very few),
and besides there was the other goal: to buy the field and so preserve
the mighty sweeping view.

So knowing the house and the field were owned by two of kin,
and the second house without the barn would face a market thin,
it was fluent Jane who did the talking, stood her ground and made it clear
for the house without the field there'd be no interest here.
And in the end we did succeed, got the land for which we cared,
but when we came to see the deeds—how house and field price had been shared—
we saw that seller, who deal agreed, her brothers' cut had pared!

7

Our double life had thus begun—English city, hamlet French;
I wasn't sure of what we'd won until I sat on sunny bench,
mug in hand by wall of house, squinting at two buzzards high
on their morning hunt for mouse, calling out with mewing cry.
They spiral up into the blue, two hazy dots becoming one,
and then the ever-tightening screw is suddenly undone
the wings-in death drop has begun
a swoop to earth from out of the sun.

… long seconds pass … then up from the grass
come beating wings lifting talon load, one strong flap takes it over the road
across the fields, past church tower, showing all Creation who has the power,
then descending in one long glide, behind the ridge as if to hide
the gloating and gorging on gory prize.
It's put on for me right under my eyes,
and any time I can watch such shows
until light fades and the slow day goes.

As evening darkens into night,
a dusky bat unnerves me,
flitting close at shoulder height
a bird that's not a bird I see in high-speed mothy flutter
split seconds just before it darts beneath the barn roof gutter
through the doorway over carts long abandoned from before.
I go inside with torch in hand to discover there are many more;

high above on beams they band, jostling bunches leering down,
all pointy ears and monkey faces: a collectively unfriendly frown.

They do not like me being there, so I step away, turn off my light
and back towards the house repair, to let these gargoyles have the night.

But I'll not let them have it all and stay leaned out in cool night air
mid bedtime reach to close the shutters, hoping I'll hear the owls out there,
and over the crickets' slow background beat, I hear far off on hillside right
the four-note call from darkest woods, soon echoed left in moonlight bright.
The night watch has called; I know all is well.
Time to turn in now, on good thoughts to dwell.

8

We came to like Arsène with his quietly nodded hallo,
though he'd never much to tell, cycling slow behind his trio.
Time stopped when he came walking past, wooden rake upon his shoulder,
stone-sharped scythe to cut the grass, seeming never to grow older.

His picture Jane once painted of him walking home one eve,
three cows and dog beside him, the lane about to leave.
As they turned into his farmyard we'd had a happy thought,
perhaps he'd like his portrait: his likeness nicely caught;
we discreetly took a photo for Jane to work from with her brush
at her studio in Cambridge as there wasn't any rush.

We put it in a wooden frame and brought it back in spring,
gave it to him and explained it was just a little thing.
He looked at it quite keenly, then said with farmer's pride
that one's Margot, that one's Bijoux—there's that mark upon her side.
We wondered what he'd do with it: would he hang it on the wall?
prop it up on top of shelf, not show it anywhere at all?

9

We and the bats are not alone in making this place home,
as well as mice, all kinds of bugs, around us redstarts roam,
perching here then darting there, they never seem to tire
of flying from tree to bush and back again, then up to telephone wire,
in and out the 'tween-stone cracks in the lichen-oranged wall,
with a nod of the head, red flick of tail, they so beguile us all.

Every spring they come to us to raise another brood,
from hotter lands much further south, it's here there's fledgling food.
For five times fifty years and more this has been their family seat,
so I mentally doff my cap to them whenever we re-meet.
It pleases me to see them here and to know that when I'm gone,
they'll be coming back each year and together our lines go on.

10

Our doorstep stands as high as Snowdon above the level sea,
two peaks rise up each side of us, though it's only one we see,
they add another thousand feet and can disappear in cloud
when the sky comes down all damp and grey and wraps us in its shroud,
at other times the sun's so hot it burns right through your skin;
it's then we seek the shade of trees or else retreat within.

Light north wind can bring good weather (and the worst one can recall),
white wool clouds float on the blue, leaves don't try to wave at all;
it's when the wind swings round from south, we know we're in for change,
Mistral-like blowing hard for days with not a cloud in range.

It can snow in May, be warm in June, rain for days on end,
then stay so dry for several weeks the trees themselves will bend.
It's a mountain climate we are told, three forces here are sent:
Med from south, Maritime from west, the rest from Continent.

Warm or cool? we need to know what the day will have in store,
so we have a huge thermometer hung just inside the door,
though with stone walls the house inside stays pretty much the same,
keeping fireside warmth in winter and summer heat more tame.

When winter piles against the door, they mobilise the snow plough,
no matter where you live, how deep it is, they'll get to you somehow.
Winter walks bring wondrous things such as icicles hung on trees,
lolloping hare tracks on the snow, the deep silence of the freeze.

The winter here seems to last for ever, its dead hand gripping the hills,
when suddenly the fields catch fire, light up, and blaze with daffodils,
buds are seen, there are hints of green, the air is humming with promise,
old meadows take on a youthful hue, getting ready for bees to kiss,
blue tits get busy, our redstarts appear preparing to raise some young,
goldfinches dart among the pines, from every twig a song is sung.

Full summer brings great cumulus clouds towering into the blue,
as hot air from lower lands climbs up to visit us too;
it's then that great storms often threaten, looming black and overgrown,
though often they just pass us by, thundering eastward to the Rhone.

By September all is calming down and there comes a lovely light
slanting gold over fields and woods, it's an evening whisky sight.
Across the glinting grass from our neighbours' chimney pile,
a curling blue of wispy smoke greets us like a smile.
At this hour we also need to light a fire before we sup:
fragrant ash and spitting pine keep us warm 'til we go up.

Not many people came to call on our neighbour old Arsène,
whether he'd many friends at all it was much beyond our ken.
Young Élise at the end of track brought him dishes of hot food,
there would perhaps be some scraps for all his cats that mewed.

Every Tuesday morning, Arsène went out in his small car
heading for the Saint-Jeures road, which wasn't very far.
We'd been told it was to meet some folk, the reason for him to go,
but whether to buy or sell or just to chat, we simply didn't know.

Where family was concerned, though, it was a rather different matter,
he'd been known to hide from Adrienne when she came with sister's natter,
for it was Jane she then went round to see when she couldn't find her brother;
she thought it odd not to find him home, but Jane couldn't blow his cover!

When his other sister came to stay, we asked them all to tea:
Arsène said nought, she seemed pleased, accepting with alacrity.
Just a simple do out on the grass—we put a folding table there—
Madame brought her partner too, a certain Monsieur Grandrivière.
'Mr Bigriver' was very proud of his unusual name,
telling us all more than once not many had the same.

We were waiting for Arsène who was coming a little late,
eventually he walked slowly in, resigned now to his fate.
His sister had surely been at work, tried hard to make him neat:
in place of his old shoes or clogs, bedroom slippers on his feet.
They gave him little comfort, though, for he wore expression grim,
it was clear that all this dressing up just simply wasn't him!

12

Le Puy-en-Velay is our capital, lying westwards from us here;
only forty minutes' drive away, it soon became quite near.
From a long way off, you can easily see two tall spikes of rock
and striped cathedral of Sainte Marie to which pious and curious flock.
One rock holds high Madonna and Child, on the other is perched a chapel,
to which visitors up cliff steps do file and with vertigo must grapple.
Another pillar standing high is Saint Joseph de Bon Espoir,
his beckoning hand and babe close by welcome pilgrims from afar.
We are always taken with surprise, whenever we come back,
how high rears up the rocky rise of Forteresse de Polignac;
its massive keep stares over the land watching all approaches,
ready to repel any fighting band or … welcome tourist coaches.

If you want to watch the world go by, the Place du Plot's the place to go:
under café shades when the sun's up high, you can feel its magic as time goes slow.
Cracked shutters hung on bright-paint walls look down on oldest mart in France,
clatter and chatter from centuries call; this place isn't special just by chance.

Hurrying past or strolling through, people come in all shape and size:
Ponots, tourists, some like us two — quasi-locals in disguise.
The old, the young, the weak, the strong, they all come here to walk or wait,
including those whose life's gone wrong because of cards dealt out by fate.
For those whose minds are troubled or must live their lives in wheelchairs,
or stumble by all huddled, they'll find Le Puy is always theirs;
for it doesn't matter who you are, what you've done or where you've been,
this quirky town will set no bar and will surely take you in.

13

The first hint we got house two was haunted came when Jane was made aware,
while hard at work upon a painting, of someone coming up the stair;
thinking it was me returning, she half turned upon her chair
but realized after briefly waiting, that nobody was there.

We thought little of it, told no one else, until two friends came down to stay;
they had this house all to themselves (it was most convenient in that way).
For in the morning one remarked, as they joined us for some coffee,
that in the night he was sure there'd been, not the two of them, but three.
A female presence, quite benign, he explained to us in detail,
this caused some mirth, a raised eyebrow, as he was middle aged and male!
but when the son of another friend, distinguished scientist no less,
came out one morning with similar tale, we then decided to confess
that remarkably he wasn't the first who'd felt some one else was there,
despite not having heard the story of what our friend had said last year.

So it seemed we'd got ourselves a ghost who had made the second house her home,
not scary at all, even nice to think we had our very own *fantôme*.
If more proof was needed, it came quite soon—the fourth piece of evidence—
as another guest, un-briefed by us, reported on a 'presence.'

So now we needed to figure out who she might be, what she might do.
We knew the year this house was built: it was only 1932,
but it had replaced an older cottage, pulled down to usher in the new,
an ancient thatched-roofed *chaumière*, half the barn built with it, too.

This half barn still stands today, later extended to take cows more,
but nothing remains of *chaumière*, save the lintel over the door.

In a certain light towards the end of day, the shadows form a sign:
a date appears on this old stone—1749.
Halfway through Louis XV's reign, forty years to Revolution,
here did a woman die without her final absolution?

It's hard to find the records of who lived where and when.
We heard there'd been a household numbering eleven,
who lived in the old half of the barn, their stock behind partitions.
On the floor above the hay was stacked; life was hard in such conditions.

We heard of a ghost not far away who lived in an old farm building;
it was a new friend who took us there and in us was now confiding.
At this empty house overgrown with weeds, this lady could sense the ghost,
but she couldn't tell us who he was or why he didn't leave his post.

As time went by we sometimes wondered if our ghost would show again,
but we heard no more reports of her; she had moved beyond our ken.
Though we did have some amusement when our daughter's teenage friends
were afraid to use a particular room, in case the ghost they might offend!

It would be many years before we learned
whether with us she was still interned.

14

One day we learned of a curious thing, how Arsène had fallen out
with widow Monette who lived close by, almost within a shout.
On this little stretch of road, they'd been the only two,
so they knew each other very well and talked as neighbours do.

It was all about a fattened pig now destined to be sausage,
that Arsène was chasing round his room and up and down the passage.
He'd got his hand around its tail but pig was through the door,
kicking over water pail, Arsène slipping on the floor.
Down he went on flagstones hard with the pig upon him too;
the squealing weight broke his leg—there was little he could do.

On kitchen floor he lay for hours and he claimed he'd made a call
to near Monette to summon help; she said her phone rang not at all.

Dawn came up, no help had come, so he searched about for wood,
put together a makeshift splint for his leg as best he could;
later, he'd act it out for us—the drama so we could see
his struggle to get across the yard to his little *sans permis*.
With greatest effort he forced his leg, stiff and swollen, inside the car,
then off he wobbled up the hill to find the folk who lived not far.

They drove him to the hospital in the city of Puy-en-Velay;
it wouldn't take them very long, being only twenty miles away.
His parting words as they left him there were *make sure you find that pig,*

it would be criminal to lose the meat on a bestiole *that big.*
He couldn't go home and finish off what he'd started night before,
he'd just have to lie in bed and wait 'til doctors wanted him no more.

Arsène spent weeks in hospital, thinking about his bacon,
until at last his leg was mended and homeward he was taken.
He went off eager to find his pig, but in this was sadly beaten,
finally told by his helpful 'friends' by them it had been eaten!

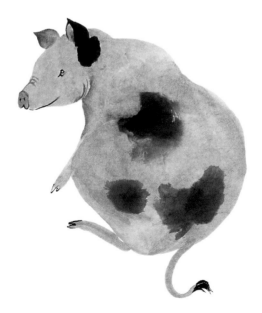

15

A mile or two from our door
is the wood called Bois des Dames,
where young daughters of the nobles
vowed devotion to the Lamb.
Secluded high on the Meygal *massif*,
on the edge of the forest they dwelled,
but here they fell prey to marauding wolves,
though prayers were sung and rosaries held.
And from time to time the convent would lose
a Sister or servant to the hungry packs,
the poor girls attacked in kitchen fields
or as they carried wood home upon their backs.

With winters long and deep snow cold,
the nuns endured the hardest of times,
but it was seventy years 'til their order decided
they should surely live in gentler climes.
Their pact with God hadn't asked them to suffer
or expect to go young to the tomb,
so the convent was left to the wolves and the crows
and the nuns moved down to Bellecombe,
a few miles away and by the same brook,
but warmer and away from the woods,
where trout could be caught and food easily grown;
there'd be more smiles from under the hoods.

In anno domini 1210
this propitious change took place.
Some decades on an abbey was built,
and the convent expanded apace.

One abbesse Margeurite showed too little restraint
and so from the abbey was banned;
she became the friend of gangster Grimoard,
who was the chief of a brigand band.
He tried to restore Margeurite as Abbesse,
but to this men-at-arms put a stop;
they imprisoned Grimoard, but a new gang was formed
with his moll Marguerite at the top.
After Grimoard escaped, they went again for the abbey
and dragged the poor nuns from their beds,
but this was too much for one of his men,
and he stabbed Grimoard until dead.
It took royal intervention to restore as abbesse,
Catherine, who'd been chased away;
after this the abbey would quieten down,
and the nuns could peacefully pray.

In Revolution year the abbey was closed
and the nuns dispersed all around;

within a year or two the mobs attacked
and pulled the whole building down.
Eight hundred years of history in ruins,
save just the barn and stable,
a chalice or two, some entries in records;
the abbey's long passed into fable.
It's now a mossy mound of stoical stones
and forlorn fragments of walls,
buried under roots are the rooms of the nuns,
long gone are the high-roofed halls.

If you go up to the 'Wood of the Ladies,'
you'll hear the trees sigh for the sad and bereft,
but of the first nuns' home you'll find no trace;
it is only their name they have left.

16

Three dozen cats Arsène once had, together with some goats,
all fed on scraps of this or that, judging by their coats.
Then came the time when he decided he really had too many,
he thought he'd offer them for free, but enquiries there weren't any,
despite the splendid notice, kindly drawn by Jane,
and nailed upon a wooden post that stood beside the lane.
We feared that passers-by who saw it, even though they sought a cat,
would take one look at where he lived and then with shock react.

Once one of his goats came trotting down, heading for our door,
where fine geraniums stood in pots—a blaze of colour to adore.
Attention—il est méchant!, sister Vermorel cried out
from the safety of her balcony and she left us in no doubt,
but too late!—the goat had made its move, its practised act of theft,
for after one enormous bite, not a single flower was left!
Then, adding insult to the injury, it seemed to say in fun,
red petals dangling from its mouth, *just look what I have done!*

Never mind, it was fun to tell stories such as this
when people asked us how it was in our rural bliss.

17

We now have to talk the politics of owning a second home;
in Britain it's often criticised: *the young can't call one house their own.*

Our set up here cannot big be called—one old barn, two houses small—
but standing with five acres round, it covers quite a lot of ground
and since we're not here all year through (we have a house in England too),
is it wrong to have so much when others simply can't have such?
We think the answer is probably not, for an empty house or a vacant plot
are not round here hard to find and several more for sale are signed.

We used local artisans and builders to restore, repair, maintain aplenty,
when it may have stayed for years uncared-for, damp and bleakly empty.
Old-restored or newly-built, second homes round here are everywhere;
it's a long-held French tradition to have a *maison secondaire.*

Our big field in front is used for hay, for which we charge no rent,
being happy that it's farmer-managed, so there's no argument against.
The other thing to keep in mind, and these are the clinching facts:
we use little public funds but pay a full year's worth of tax!
So we believe we put more in than ever we take out;
after all this is our choice, and of its worth we have no doubt.

18

From old Le Puy the faithful trekked
to Compostelle's St Jaques,
a weary trudging pilgrim sect,
their souls upon their backs.
Many today still take this road,
some seeking answers to life's pain.
I hope that they can shed their load
with the knowledge that they gain.

They leave Le Puy's ancient heart
of narrow alley and cobbled street,
old stone arches, carved door art,
all leading up to God's high seat.
Sainte Marie looks down on red-roofed cluster,
black Madonna enshrined within,
ebony face amid golden lustre,
eyes that spear through those who sin.

We can be sure there came to see her,
when Louis Quinze was king of France,
people from across the Allier,
with eyes cast down and furtive glance,
imploring her to end their curse,
just a donkey ride away.
Things in Gévaudan could not be worse:
evil itself had come to stay.

Shepherd children didn't come home,
single travellers weren't seen again,
distant sightings of strange forms,
quite unknown to the eyes of men.
People just vanished, it would seem,
'til a goat girl would ghastly find
the torn-off heads staining red a stream
and run shrieking home out of her mind,
tripping on tree roots, stumbling on stone,
certain the Beast can't be far behind,
terrified out there on her own.

It bounded out from forest dark,
leapt upon victims from the rear,
all foaming jaws, satanic bark,
blood-red eyes and huge as a bear.
An alien lion or monstrous dog
or half man half wolf some swore it to be,
it was the rustle of leaves on half-buried log,
the shape half-seen behind the tree.
Each kill was enquired by marquis and bishop
then, if proved, written in record,
but nothing it seems could make it stop:
not musket balls, lances or swords.

At least the Beast in pain could scream,
averred young Marie-Jeanne Valet:
when walking through woods beside a stream,

she had heard from behind, a bay.
She turned around, tight with fear,
to find the Beast towering over her head;
she managed to hold up her makeshift spear,
plunging it into that chest with dread.
The Beast let out a horrible cry,
pawed at its wound and with stagger and sway,
rolled into the water flowing fast by
and brave Marie got safely away.

Once a young lad protecting his sister
fought the Beast off with a knife to the shoulder;
it bounded away after it missed her,
but from then on it became ever bolder,
stalking the hills for mile after mile,
crossing vast tracts in a single day,
marking all Gévaudan with its kills,
afraid of nothing it found in its way.

The Beast then attacked full seven men,
but they stayed close in and successfully fought.
When the king heard this story he decreed
it was the State's duty to get the Beast caught.
So he sent his finest hunter in chief
with a mounted cavalcade,
who searched the land but to no avail,
though through the winter they stayed.

Wolf hunters were sent but had no better luck,
attacks continued spreading more terror,
so in the end the king had to accept
he should send his own *arquebus* bearer,
who, in late 1765,
tracked a big beast, which he finally shot.
It was hot lead balls that brought it down
—just a large wolf, a monster not.

The people waited, but as months went by
and there was no more blood on the rocks,
they breathed again, went about their work,
sent out their children again with the flocks,
but within a year came the chilling news,
talked of throughout the land:
a small boy had been found with his throat ripped out
and not by human hand.

Their nightmare fears were horribly right:
the Beast after all had not been caught,
despite the king's triumphant hunter
showing its carcass off to the court.
Some of the locals had humbly noticed,
when the soldiers came back from their raid,
there was no scar upon the Beast
that could have been made by a blade.

So those fine soldiers with all their fine steeds,
who'd taken their hay and most of their food,
during the leanest of winters to meet their needs
(was it not, indeed, for the wretches' own good
the king sending soldiers to get rid of the Beast?)
had all been for nought, and now they're afraid
there is no other way, they must believe their priest,
who says it's God's wrath for being disobeyed.

You know full well you're living in sin,
debauched and immoral, from grace you did fall,
so roared their righteously thundering church:
the Beast has been sent to punish you all.

A message went off to the king and his court,
pleading anew for his help with this terror,
but he thought these peasants were asking too much;
his hunter had killed it, there was no error
—hadn't the Beast been shown stuffed in Versailles?
So no soldiers appeared and the killings went on,
until a man came forward, a strange look in his eye:
one of the brothers Chastel—this one was Jean.

They kept to themselves out of people's way,
breeding war dogs, maybe wolf-crosses too;
whatever it was the brothers got up to,
wasn't too good if the rumours were true.

Jean Chastel shrugged off the sceptical stares,
picked up his gun and went off alone.
Back some hours later he said it was over;
hard to believe what he'd done on his own.

For the enormous wolf they saw for themselves
had been killed with a single shot to the head
(Jean said it was the balls forged of pure silver
which meant that he couldn't fail to deliver).
They also saw a knife scar on its shoulder:
it was the Beast alright, and now it was dead.
From that day on there were no more slaughters,
no more sightings of terrible creatures,
or hopeless searching for dead daughters,
faces of strangers with fear-frozen features.

So a hero now was Jean Chastel,
this man who had killed the Beast;
a celebration was held to honour him,
but he declined to join in with their feast.
From that day on, he seemed to change,
seen at church for the first time ever,
hours alone down on his knees,
hands clasped tight in silent prayer,
eyes fixed hard on altar window,
gazing up at Christ's enthronement,
praying for the souls the Beast had taken
—or was all this Jean's atonement?

As the years went by, the questions came:
wolves don't hunt alone but in packs;
were unused to people; would hide from them,
not seek them out for fearless attacks.
How had Chastel managed the miracle,
when others before him had failed?
What special knowledge did Jean possess
so he knew he'd return unassailed?
Had Chastel in fact known the Beast before?
Was dog-wolf breeding a disaster?
Did he know if he whistled the Beast would obey
and come running home to its master?

We will never know what really went on,
and it's best not to heed those tales,
when one ventures abroad into old Gévaudan
to follow its dark forest trails.
The legacy of those terrible times
stays with us to this day;
now and then reports come in—
a wolf has been seen, they say.
Pas de loup mais toujours la peur,
a recent headline ran;
it seems that it will never die
—*la Bête* in mind of man.

19

It's in September that I go looking for the yellow *Chanterelle*,
that grows upon the slopes of Lisieux in a boggy grassy dell.
An old acquaintance showed me this spot many years ago,
in sunny glades amid dark firs these mushrooms like to grow.

My family I've brought up here, daughter, brother and granddaughters,
making sure I leave the car how my old acquaintance taught us:
some distance down the forest road, away from little track
that leads us to this secret place and (less surely) takes us back.
He told me that it has been known that cars without the 'forty-three'
can strangely sometimes get flat tyres, if parked too close where all can see.
I'm happy to say our GB plate gives us good immunity:
our car is always left untouched underneath the tree.

It always takes me half an hour, often more, before I find
those grey-brown heads on orange stems that from the grass I must unwind.
Then I see them everywhere, hiding away at the foot of trees,
under rotting logs in dappled shade, tightly clumped in twos and threes.
I push on through thickets, half crouched down, oblivious of the cost
in tearing clothes and poked eyeballs, until I realise I am lost!
I seldom find the path again, forgetting the way to go,
all I do is head downhill 'til I meet the road below.

So back I come triumphantly, my basket brimming with *girolles*,
sometimes defying the general view of local 'opinion polls'.

Not many seen this year, they say, *as it's been too dry too long,*
so when I turn up with my little gift, they know they got it wrong!
I'm pleased to be able to share with them my fresh-from-forest prize
(how is it that a foreigner here can be so mushroom-wise?)

20

Clink of glasses, children's play talk, laughter in the air,
back and forth across the table, conversation everywhere.
Our group of neighbours, who are friends, sit together in the evening,
all ages (one to eighty-eight) understand each other's meaning.

This is the French *apéritif*, a marvellous tradition,
so comfortably relaxing, no social inhibition.
Titbits are fine, home-cooked or not, it isn't like our English way:
after midday lunch is finished, big meals are over for the day.
No dressing up, come when you can, it really doesn't matter,
bring the children, they'll join the adults amid the steady chatter;
they'll stay up late, curl up on laps, and be parlayed with by all,
even teenagers will join the throng, one eye on iPhone call.

It's not a meal exactly, but more than just a snack,
some's been in the oven, some fresh-toasted on the rack.
Piled plates appear at intervals as the merry time goes on,
emptying progressively, 'til nearly all of it has gone.
Then we will sit together for another hour or two,
it's the company that matters, food and drink are just the glue.

We'll find out who has just come back or gone away elsewhere,
who's had twins or lost a dog or has fallen down the stair,
why the woodsmen are so worried about the lessening rain,
why the town hall's taking ages to repair that broken drain.
We'll wonder what on earth Monsieur Macron thinks he's doing

and whether it's Mrs Merkel Mrs May should be a-wooing,
if Trump is really mad or perversely very clever;
never mind, try this one out, it's a nice one from the cellar.

We think we're rather lucky to have such people near,
who willingly include us in things they hold quite dear,
seem always pleased to see us, even though we're birds of passage,
give us bags of homegrown veg, some for Cambridge carriage.

We've been coming here for so long now we know almost all the places
where one can find this or that and we also know the faces
of who is who and when it was they used to live up there,
who's their cousin and their brother, the name of their *grand-mère*.
People sometimes seem surprised that we seem to know so much;
they rack their brains for a name, then we say it's such-and-such!
These things give us little tingles of modest pride and pleasure,
we feel that we belong a bit; it's not just lazy leisure.

21

From our crowded English isle,
it went some time ago, that feeling of the open road,
meet no other car for miles.

Setting off on fine bright mornings
from last night's *logis* stop; flickering sun through leaves above,
driving under tree shade awnings.

The best part of our French commute
up and down the hexagon: taking D-marked country roads
before we join the *autoroute*.

The stops that split our journeys whole
meld into one kaleidoscope of silent streets in little towns,
as we take after supper stroll.

Occasionally we glimpse some light
behind half-open shutters; we wonder who is living there
and if everything's alright.

We retrace our steps to the inn
and think about next day, look at the map, plot a route
check when breakfast will begin.

To go past Paris east or west
is the only big decision. The first is faster but not as scenic;
to reach Auvergne from west is best.

Heading south to Clermont-Ferrand
over rising rolling farmland, we make our routine ice-cream stop
at the busy Aire des Volcans.

We no longer crawl through old Brioude
though it's pretty as a picture; it's Le Puy-en-Velay that then puts us
in happy home-returning mood.

22

The higher slopes of our hills are clothed in evergreen,
but lower down the trees are mixed, and winter leafless patches seen.
Above the fields the woods are dense, but it wasn't always so:
old postcards show our valley bare not so long ago.
Late in the 19th century, there were twice the people here,
tiny farms scratched on the hillsides, little houses everywhere.

A short hard life it must have been, though soil is good and will provide,
it's full of stones which can break bones as they're heaved off to the side.
And of course the season's short to grow much grass or crop,
so since those times most left behind homes upon hilltop,
but if you climb among the trees, you can often find their traces:
ruined shelters, roots of walls, stone-paved lanes in steeper places.

At the hamlet crossroads, a kind of chapel stands,
but these *assemblées* aren't for worship and found only in these lands.
Many years ago it was the home of our community's *béate*,
a spinster whose main role it was to teach children as they sat
in the room downstairs and had to do catechism with good grace,
and after that the local women would gather to make lace.
The *béate* would also tend the ill and comfort those near end,
ring the bell upon her roof when there were meetings to attend.

For two hundred years, these *demoiselles* supplied the only social service
for lonely hamlets in distant hills and it more or less came gratis.
The people themselves would have to ask for a *béate* to be sent their way,

if the priest agreed, then they would build the house where she would stay.
She wasn't paid but had food and fuel, a table and some chairs,
was given a bed and one wardrobe for her single room upstairs.

And so she'd spend all her days, serving those who lived close to,
and in return she'd be assured of her they'd take care too.
It's been fifty years since the last *béate* was working in these parts;
she must have hoped that when she went she'd stay on in people's hearts.

For many years our own *assemblée* slowly became a ruin,
then an enterprising neighbour thought that something needed doing;
he wrote to the mayor who agreed to repair the roof and crumbling wall,
so the *assemblée* could once again serve some purpose for us all.
A little museum, a place to meet, somewhere to stage a play?
But apart from a talk and the odd event, nothing's come to stay.
It's also become apparent that a fungus has moved in;
it's got the timbers in rotting grip—we hope it will not win.

So in this modern day and age it's hard to find a role
for what was once this hamlet's heart and maybe too its soul.

23

The people of the land of *sucs* are known for their warm welcomes,
don't hesitate to help a stranger,
and warn of any danger.
They're also independent and even tell us they can be stubborn,
perceived slights are never forgotten,
relationships go rotten.
After families have fallen out among their very own,
they'll not speak to each other again,
once-strong blood ties left to wane.

It seems to me this is just the same as in families everywhere,
if what is measured is love received,
it's easy to feel aggrieved.
We heard a tale of two sisters whose aged mother had passed,
only one thing of value she had,
it was all a little sad.
A large *armoire* of chestnut wood, a fine wardrobe handed down,
but whose clothes now should be put inside,
after poor mother had died?
Each sister said *our mother said the wardrobe was meant for me,*
since Maman had other things for you;
but the other said *not true.*

They sought legal advice and back it came, much as one might expect:
one sister buys out the other's share
or both of them sell elsewhere.

But it seemed this answer wouldn't do, each sister wanted it for herself;
their bickering lasted for ages,
on many written pages.
Until at last their lawyer said, half in jest half in despair,
you'll just have to have it cut in two;
yes, they said, *that's what we'll do!*

So the lawyer was instructed to oversee the separation,
make sure the joiner didn't fiddle:
his saw went down the middle.
New wood was then affixed to cover both the open sides,
two *demi-armoires* now in effect,
just left or right to select.

And both the sisters then hauled away with grim-faced satisfaction,
mementos of their dearest mother,
each one just like the other.
Worth almost next to nothing: just narrow cupboards absurdly tall;
but better by half than having nothing, if your sister got it all.

24

Bread and cheese are life essentials,
nowhere more so than in France;
a meal without long loaf of bread
—one simply doesn't take the chance.
And always put before dessert,
fromage is offered soft or dry;
again your meal can't be complete,
if you don't give the cheese a try.

In every town and village here,
boulangeries are their warming hearts,
with the *mairie*, *café* and *épicerie*,
they are their vital parts.
Just two miles away in our Araules,
delicious bread is made,
and golden croissants so buttery,
which for anything I'd trade.
Each morning people make the trip,
some on foot, most by car,
but very few (like me) will grip
a cycle handlebar.

I can't help thinking of what it costs
in carbon-nox pollution

per kilometre-gram of *pain*:
it's not a good solution!
But what can rural dwellers do
who don't live near but far instead
and where there is no baker too,
how will they get their nice fresh bread?
So despite my eco-smirking smugness
at those with blue gas in their wakes,
I can't help admire and love the way
France drives miles for better bakes.

On golden mornings with small white clouds
puffy fluffing across the blue,
I cycle up to the high wide sky,
past shining grass still wet with dew,
bump onto the road at top of ridge
and start my plunge down other side,
as forested dome of Achon *suc*
comes up around the bend I ride.
Freewheeling roar of rushing wind,
gathering speed, I'm in full flight,
tears streaming from my close-slit eyes,
I'm over the crossroads at lowest height,
climbing again towards Araules,
slower and slower as momentum goes,

pedalling on to pass the square,
between grey houses roofed with *lauzes*.

I reach the baker's, smell fresh bread,
sort out my money, arrange my *sac*;
the journey home I must now tackle,
bread and croissants in pack on back.

Pick the place to go lowest gear,
start the long deep breathing haul,
doggedly grinding back up the hill,
past shattered house where storm did call.
A car comes down, then a milk tanker,
shining and swaying like a boat at sea,
roaring round road swell, in a second it's past,
thousands of litres whoosh by me
(it's important here to bring the milk in fast!).

I'm now in the trees, tall farmhouse on left,
though of anyone there I never see sign,
but the place is well kept, flowers planted round side,
sometimes washing hung out on the line.
Six chairs round a table outside I saw once,
and even two loungers laid under the trees,
blue tent to sleep two, maybe chattering kids,
cousins from Paris or perhaps Pyrenees?

As I go puffing by I imagine their lives,
then one day in mid-August everything's gone,
the farmhouse is back to its usual shy self;
it would be rude to enquire, so I go pedalling on.

At last I'm on top, gear up, pick up speed,
swing off the road and take sandy track,
I see Lisieux's bald pate peering over the trees;
I'm looking forward to breakfast when I get back.

25

Cycling in France is a serious sport that's always on the go,
especially here where steep hill climbs so test leg muscles more.
Every cyclist seen around these parts is dressed from head to toe
in the proper kit and on machines that could be in *Le Tour*.

In year 2017, this race came here again,
streaming past the turtle rock on the road from Boussoulet.
Our son and in-law brother, themselves both cyclists keen,
flew out here to see it all in just three days of stay.

The way I'm dressed upon my bike must leave much to be desired,
at least compared with all the others who cycle through these lands,
no Lycra shirt, no too-tight shorts, just not properly attired
as I wear long trousers stuffed in socks, no gloves upon my hands.

And as for my velocipede, on that we needn't dwell!
but then all I'm doing is getting bread (and sometimes cheese as well).

26

Our valley's portrait is a study in green,
with the odd yellow streak for the cereal ones sees
and a few flecks of rock grey painted between
broad strokes of light grass as well as dark trees.
Hot summers may retouch the grass into straw
until the rain returns to paint it again,
dabbling on green to make it look like before,
bringing back colour to the face of the glen.

When clouds smudge the hills with a wash of smoke grey
and our rock-perched turtle swims off in the mist
and we almost lose sight of those over the way,
we know that for hours this fog will persist.
As we're high in Haute-Loire, the nights can be chilled
and so in the mornings there's often rich dew,
on broad blades of grass pure water's distilled
and the land stays verdant all the year through.

It's good for the cattle, scattered everywhere
on the pasture below and all up the slopes,
big Charolais bulls, long-horned cows from Saler,
their coffee-coloured calves being farmers' best hopes.
Mountain toughness from cow, fine beef from the bull,
though some want good milkers and rear other breeds,
so the tanker that calls can be filled up to 'full'
and the dairy in Araules has all the milk that it needs.

The dairy was founded just after the war
by Jules and Madeleine Gerentes,
who up until then collected eggs from the farms
and other products the markets might want.
Asked by the farmers if they could also take milk,
they decided to make butter and cheese,
and put up a dairy in the heart of Araules
as a family-run *entreprise*.

Now seventy years on the dairy has grown,
processing milk from a hundred herds;
prizes have been won by the *Bleu de Lisieux*,
a cheese with a taste judged superb.
The dairy is central to our local economy,
it's why many valley farms are still going,
along with a sawmill for pines from the forests,
which are then left alone for re-growing.

The dairy's yellow tower is a landmark,
rising above the encircling grey roofs;
unlike Queyrière's dead stub of volcano,
of energy today this pillar is proof.
It means that here's still a good place to live,
one sees not just old, but young working faces;
the downside is the new sheds that appear,
block-ugly constructed in the prettiest places.

Our house search extended to northern Ardèche,
where the landscape's 'unspoilt,' old hamlets 'pristine,'
but farms are abandoned, the fields are unkempt,
it's all second homes—no residents seen.
We'd rather have the sight and also the sound
of people around who work for a living,
and though sheds may go up and trees come down,
it's good that these hills are going on giving.

27

Though Arsène could look like Worzel Gummidge,
a quiet dignity he mustered;
this was evident when one day
two men from EDF got flustered.
Onto our land behind our house,
they just marched straight in from off their truck
to clear some branches high above
where a fallen cable had got stuck.

They pushed and pulled to no avail,
then Arsène said something to them,
they took one look at this 'country bumpkin'
and proceeded to ignore him.
They struggled on for quite some time
until Arsène produced his rake,
without a word he raised it up
and cable off the branch did take.

With one deft movement, he'd achieved
what they'd failed to do in half an hour;
Arsène then calmly left the scene
to let the two restore the power.

28

One summer's day I sit in the sun,
looking up the valley to the turtle tor
and become aware that the drifting clouds
have slowed so much they move no more,
held fast in a sea that's upside down,
ice-floe white frozen on blue.
All is still, there is no sound,
no aeroplane drone, no buzzard mew.

The hills have no age, time is just waiting,
the planet itself has stopped rotating,
held for eternity in cosmic calm;
our valley's at peace, will come to no harm.
To fix this moment I must endeavour,
to recall at will, sustain me for ever.

Eons pass, I see a slight shimmer
in the heat haze over the field,
a tiny grass head bobs on its stem,
a redstart tail flicks a brief glimmer.
Tit wings whirr in the elderberry tree,
wood saws start a far forest buzz,
clouds resume their soft slow passage;
in that moment the turtle saw me.

The earth is turning again.

29

The high hard lands of the Haute-Loire
are home to formidable folk,
who risked their lives to keep others safe
when France bent to the Nazi yoke.
No Vichy compromise for them,
no going along with Pétain,
pointing to those of Jewish faith,
supporting their persecution.

To our very own commune of Araules,
two Jewish youngsters were sent,
brother and sister whose parents in Lyon
feared what the yellow stars meant.
They were put on a train bound for the hills
and stopping at Yssingeaux,
there they were met by pony and trap
to take them up to the plateau.

They stayed in the home of baker and wife
attended the local school,
for three good years they were hidden away,
out of reach of Vichy rule.
One day the order came from high up
that schools had to check their flock,
declare which children were 'truly' French
and which were from 'other' stock.

The young schoolteacher went through her register,
ticking as French all the names,
she came to young Stupp who, with his sister,
was out in the yard playing games.
She paused with pen in hesitant hand
for she knew what she'd pay for lying,
but took only a second to make up her mind
and bravely decide on defying.

Sixty years later, the boy wrote a book
about the remarkable trust
his parents had placed in the people here
—he called it 'The Land of the Just.'
He tells of Le Lisieux's two-headed peak,
which became a familiar sight,
how it made him feel he belonged to this place
and all in the end would be right.

Many were hidden away in these hills
in villages, hamlets and farms.
Le Chambon-sur-Lignon alone took in hundreds,
despite people's natural qualms;
but then they knew how their own forebears
had suffered because of their faith,
hounded by the state as Protestants,
they fled to somewhere more safe.

Pastor André and helper Edouard
organized the good folk of this town,
obtained forged papers and ration cards,
and sheltered refugees all around.
When the militias came calling, looking for Jews,
their quarry hid in the forests,
waiting until they heard their protectors
sing out the all clear for their guests.

Le Chambon's citizens were later honoured
by Israel's Yad Vashem,
'Righteous among Nations' is the proud title
bestowed upon all of them.

Indeed, this corner of France could claim
to be the brave heart of the nation,
for most people here refused to accept
any deal to ease Occupation.
In the same Margeride where the Beast once preyed
is a tall grey column of stone,
armed man and woman look defiantly out
over land they know is their own.

This lonely plinth stands in high regard
for those who rallied for France,
answered the call to take up their weapons,
coming out to take their chance.

This mount on Haute-Loire's western edge,
as the D-Day landings drew near,
saw the largest gathering of the *maquis*
to stop Germans going north from here.

Led by Emile Coulaudon ('Colonel Gaspard'),
the *maquis* dug in and the fighting was hard.
The Germans brought more troops to the fray
to clear the *maquis* off Mont Mouchet.
Allied air drops were planned but they never came
(in invasion confusion who was to blame?)
Under artillery fire, attacks from the air,
what had started as hope was becoming despair.

Running low on ammo, the *maquis* had to stop,
but the Germans then found when they got to the top,
though they'd forced the *maquis* to give up the fight,
they had all quietly vanished into the night.
It wasn't only the Resistance who died here for France
because the Nazis took revenge for the *maquis*' brave stance,
burning villages and farms for miles around,
cold-blooded executions staining the ground.

These proud lands of west Haute-Loire
lie forgotten now beneath the sky,
woods and pastures quiet and far,
the rest of France just passes them by.

30

Poor Leylou was a dog of very little brain,
and never got the hang of herding cows along the lane.
When his master called, he'd come hobbling to the front,
start barking at the leading cow, who'd back away and grunt,
he'd then go limping back again and 'attack' them from the rear,
nipping at the cows' legs instead of keeping clear,
never working out he should stay back at least one pace
and so was always getting kicked in almost every place.

He tried his loyal best to steer the cows along the way,
and never understood why they ignored him every day.
Though little simple Leylou never learned what he should do,
he thought he was important, a key member of the crew.

Then came the year when we returned to find Leylou was no more,
perhaps one bovine kick too many had laid him on the floor.
This dog had never been much use, however hard he tried,
but now Arsène no longer had little Leylou by his side.

31

The station at Retournac, that sits beside the Loire,
has a plaque upon its wall of war commemoration;
we noticed it the last time
we visited this station.

On a warm and sleepy afternoon, we waited for the train,
sat in shade on platform bare, not a single soul in sight;
no car went over level crossing
no one checked the signal light.

All was quiet in Retournac as we waited for our friends,
a couple coming all the way from South Australia far;
the second time we'd meet them here
at our Adelstrop on Loire.

She'd been a friend since old schooldays, he was her twelve-year partner,
tall and lanky, proper Aussie, nicest person you could meet,
charmed everyone who met him here
even strangers in the street.

Now both of them will not be back, for before the year was out,
he had left this world for ever, took the great big smile he had;
we hope she'll come here again
though our memories be sad.

32

Being seen as something of a recluse,
Arsène was rumoured to have a stash;
people saw he spent next to nothing,
but drew a pension so must have cash.
Not wanting queries from the tax man,
Arsène hid cows up in the woods,
which left just three of them to show
these were his only worldly goods.

But as it turned out, he banked his money,
had an account, and used cheque books,
but one sad day while withdrawing a pile,
this act was noticed by some crooks.
They must have reckoned they'd found *a right one 'ere*
and followed him to see where he'd driven,
they hid near his home until he went out
and they could find the money he'd hidden.

They took the money and got away with it,
said to be most of what he'd saved,
what he'd wanted this for was not too clear
—something special he'd always craved?
At least this was the story as told to us,
but he seemed to be the same Arsène,
made never a mention of his misfortune;
just didn't want to tell it again.

33

Not long back, that lady came calling
(the one who feels the presence of ghosts);
we thought she might like to look around,
it would be our turn to be the hosts.
When we set off on a brief house tour,
she said *your* fantôme's *gone and there's nothing bad*
or I couldn't have gone in through the door.
So our ghost was no more; we felt a bit sad.

We thought of our visit to the haunted farmhouse
and asked about the ghostly other,
he's gone now too, came the reply;
maybe he's searching for a brother?
But we like to think her ghost and ours
have finally found true love,
hand in hand they travel the earth,
strolling through the stars above.

34

One fine morning as I opened the shutter
I heard from below Arsène in mid mutter,
pacing back and forth, some paper held near,
he must have been waiting for us to appear.
We hurried downstairs and quickly went out
to see what his visit was really about.
He showed Jane a vet's bill to do with a cow
and said she must phone this number right now;
so what shall I say? she asked him again
but oddly our neighbour was loth to explain.

Jane got through to the vet's and made it quite clear
Arsène urgently needed the vet to come here,
but she couldn't say exactly why this was so,
which prompted a laughing *we think we know!*
It seems the good vet had come just yesterday
to put the cow of Arsène in the family way;
he must be annoyed the AI hadn't taken
and he couldn't just let his poor cow be forsaken.

Jane said *yes* to Arsène: the vet would come back,
at which Arsène just nodded and went up the track,
no mention of how bull-less calves could be bred;
in such delicate matters it was best the less said!

35

There are some little problems of which I must now speak,
certain social customs that I anticipate with gloom:
one is the greeting kiss bestowed upon the cheek,
the other is the use of *tu* and especially with whom.

Here one says hallo three times with politely-proffered kiss,
but starting with wrong side I usually decide,
and either finish up with an embarrassing near miss,
or force my startled victims to swing their faces wide.

Using *tu* is a minefield for those who are unaware
of the complicated rules and you have to take some care
not to be overfamiliar with those with years on you,
or with people who you have to say you never really knew.
And then again you can confuse those of slightly younger year,
if you *tu* them when they've *vous*-ed you—it will all sound very queer—
especially if all they're doing is just showing some veneration,
as those with whom they're talking are of an older generation.

The more you get to know people and talk gets less discreet,
there will come one day a moment when somebody will switch
from the *vous* to the *tu* the next time when you meet,
and hopefully it all goes nice and smoothly with no hitch.
But it's the next time after that which can leave you in some doubt,
when you find if they've remembered they should now be using *tu*,

and if it isn't *tu* they say, then you have to figure out
if they've simply just forgotten or would rather stick with *vous*.

So when I meet with people I haven't seen for quite a while,
I forget if we're now using *tu* or actually we're not,
so I try to make a guess and put on a casual smile,
hoping if I've got it wrong it won't matter such a lot;
and if faux pas indeed I've made, they'll just shrug and put it down
to some misunderstanding by this sometimes baffling *Anglais*,
who when he's talking French often has a puzzled frown,
and anyway it doesn't matter if he is muddling what to say!

36

We never knew if Arsène liked his life or he had hoped for something else,
maybe a friend, perhaps a wife, not to be always by himself;
then one day he did reveal as tenants looked at house behind,
he hoped indeed they'd do the deal and move in soon when all was signed.

As we shut up house and drove away, we knew Arsène was dreading
the frozen nights and ice-cold days and winter's snowy bedding.
We thought of him and bought a scarf to bring over to him next year,
perhaps he'd smile, maybe he'd laugh, at what we wanted him to wear.
But when we came back in the spring, we learned that winter was his last,
our little gift too late to bring, his need for it had sadly passed.

But I keep in mind a memory clear from his last June in early morn;
at first the sound was hard to hear through shutters that were closely drawn.
Opening them, wondering what it means, I glimpse a warming sight:
his gentle shadow hoeing beans, softly singing in the light.

He was laid to rest in local ground beside others of his name,
which has been here three hundred years, census records prove that fame.
His name's now gone for evermore, none other's quite the same;
we haven't found another like it since our neighbour he became.
His mother only spoke patois, at least that's what we were told,
from humble stock he was thought of, but his lineage was old.

We thought we'd like Jane's painting to remember Arsène by,
so we asked his niece if she could keep a helpful open eye

when clearing out his house as it could be anywhere,
but she quickly shook her head: she was sure it wasn't there.
We wondered where he'd put it, clearly not hung upon a wall
or propped upon a shelf or sill; hadn't he wanted it at all?
or maybe it was treasured, rolled in cloth to keep it clean,
tucked safely in a drawer that his niece had never seen,
for an awful lot of furniture had seemed to us tossed out,
destined for the landfill, not wanted left about.

It did seem rather odd to us it had vanished without trace,
but then that's how he ran his home, with so much in funny place.
His brother had built an apartment on the side of the old barn wall,
with hot and cold and toilet too, and that probably wasn't all.
When brother died and Arsène had moved to the house he had inherited,
in this annex would his sister stay on her visits when thought merited.
Then when the journey got too much and she could no longer just come by,
her brother filled the flat with hay: seemed the perfect place to keep it dry.

Le Puy was the furthest he'd ever been from the valley of the Auze,
all his life he'd spent round here, throughout all his highs and lows.
Its rocks and woods, its fields and streams, its villages and farms,
were all the universe he had, could hold in outstretched arms.
Up here on crystal starry nights, so brightly shines the Milky Way,
he may have thought that he was blessed, to live here in Combevieille.

Two photos are now all we have of Arsène who used to walk
twice daily past our cottage door and would sometimes stop to talk.
We felt a little privileged, being once invited in
to his humble tumbledown to which most had never been.

So with these words I've written down, we will keep refreshed our thoughts
of Arsène Lechaine who once had lived in the house that we had bought.

37

The house of Arsène looked just the same, its usual dishevelled state,
we wondered what would become of it, who would now decree its fate;
rumours began that a sale was near to make it a *gite* or *chambre d'hôtes*
and while we hoped for a family there, it wasn't as if we had a vote.

Then one day a couple came round, a very engaging pair,
they were the ones who'd be moving in and setting themselves up there.
They got to work with barely a rest, considering the time it took
to put on a new roof, remodel the inside, while keeping its period look;
all their friends and their family too seemed to become involved,
two dozen or more sitting down to lunch: the labour problem solved!

We were quietly much delighted to have such charming neighbours
who brought Arsène's house back to life; this pleasing gift they gave us.
A little boy played his part in this rejuvenating scene,
followed later by a brother: some two years are in between.
It's good to see them riding bikes all up and down the lane,
one is shy, the other bolder; the place is young again.

38

We took the road out 'tween Ollières and Achon,
came off the plateau at the end of September,
as the red town of Yssingeaux came into sight,
we knew there would be such a lot to remember.
We'd be back again in 2019,
but knew it wouldn't be quite the same,
we'd be a little more foreign than we are now,
no longer European by name.

We didn't believe this would make any difference
to all our good friends in France,
but in our hearts we felt we'd betrayed them
though we'd left nothing to chance.
In Britain we'd supported the 'Stay In' campaign,
went on marches and voted 'Remain';
when we heard the result we couldn't believe it,
felt like crying so great was the pain.

For the very first time in my whole life,
I knew how civil wars could start,
how a man could kill his neighbour or friend,
who once had a place in his heart.
My own fellow Britons had just gone and decreed
I could not stay a true European;
since they didn't want to be that themselves,
I too must be content with just Britain.

I knew as we left the valley of the Auze,
turned to look back at the skyline,
that from here on it would be harder to feel
this place was still rightfully mine.
In the last thirty years I've been everywhere,
across the whole world I'd roam,
and as did Cambridge, so Combevieille
came to be half of my home.

So we'd like to thank you all, good people,
of commune Araules and town Yssingeaux,
of Le Chambon-sur-Lignon and Saint-Étienne:
for being such welcoming friends.

Notes and Translations

Arquebus

Derived from the German *hakenbüchse*, it was a form of long gun that appeared in Europe during the 15th century. Essentially, the arquebus was larger than a musket and required a fixed rest, such as a forked stick placed in the ground, to support it when being fired.

It may have been the arquebus' capacity to discharge heavier shot than a musket that persuaded Louis xv to dispatch his sole arquebus bearer to Gévaudan in pursuit of the Beast.

Assemblée

A small building, often consisting of just one room downstairs and one upstairs, that was constructed by the local residents of hamlets and villages throughout the Velay during the 18th and 19th centuries, particularly the latter, to house their *béate*. The small bell on its roof helps to give an *assemblée* its characteristic chapel-like appearance.

Bestiole

Usually used to mean 'beast' or 'animal' (which is the sense in which Arsène Lechaine was using it), it can also mean a 'bug' or 'insect.'

Béate

In the mid-1660s, Anne-Marie Martel of Le Puy-en-Velay established the institution *Demoiselles de l'Instruction*, which might be translated in this context as 'Young Lady Teachers.' Dressed in black and wearing white caps and crucifixes, the mission of these 'lay sisters' was to teach the catechism and provide religious instruction in general to children in the remoter hamlets of the Haute-Loire and Ardèche. This movement was part of an attempt by the Catholic authorities to counter Protestantism. *Béates*, many of whom also taught lace making and sometimes, reading, writing and arithmetic and might occasionally look after the infirm and elderly, were particularly numerous in the 19th century, peaking at around 900. With the establishment of free, state-provided education by the Jules Ferry laws in the early 1880s, teaching by *béates* was forbidden, their own level of education now being deemed inadequate. Nevertheless, many *béates* continued to teach the catechism and lace making for many years thereafter, the last *béate* retiring in the 1960s.

Bourg
A market town or, if small, a village. When used in the addresses given in French telephone directories, it signifies that the address concerned is located in the actual town or village that gives its name to the commune as opposed to locations elsewhere in that commune.

Chaumière
A cottage, the name derived from *chaume* (thatch).

Chanterelle
Chanterelle is the common name of several species of fungi in the genera *Cantharellus*, *Craterellus*, *Gomphus*, and *Polyozellus*. They are among the most popular of edible wild mushrooms and include the girolle (*Cantharellus*

cibarius). The French name for the mushroom referred to in the poem is *Chanterelle Jaunâtre*. While quite tasty, this is not considered to be as delicious as the *Chanterelle Comestible*.

Demoiselle
Young lady.

Gévaudan
An ancient region of France, formerly located in the southern province of Languedoc and corresponding to most of the modern department of Lozère and part of the department of Haute-Loire to the north of Lozere. Gévaudan ceased to exist after the French Revolution of 1789.

La Micheline
The name given by people in the Haute-Loire to the light, diesel-powered autorail trains that were in service during the post-war period. Strictly speaking, La Micheline was a train introduced by the Michelin company in the 1930s, which had wheels fitted with pneumatic tyres. The red and white Haute-Loire autorail trains were popularly called Michelines because of their resemblance to the original ones (thought without the tyres).

Lauze

A large, flat stone, looking rather like a thick, rough slate, that is used for roofing. In the Haute-Loire, most *lauzes* were fashioned by cleaving the volcanic rock Phonolite. The last *lauze* quarry in the Haute-Loire stopped working in the middle of the last century. As with thatch in the UK, *lauze* is still in demand for repairing or renovating old roofs. However, it is relatively expensive to do this and so when in need of a major overhaul, a *lauze* roof these days is often replaced by a tiled roof. Phonolite is so called because a suspended sheet of it makes a melodic ring when tapped with a hard object such as a hammer or another piece of rock.

Maquis

Rural guerrilla bands of French resistance fighters, called *maquisards*, set up during the Nazi occupation of France in World War II. Initially, they were composed of men and women who had escaped into the mountains to avoid conscription into Vichy France's *Service du travail obligatoire* ('Compulsory Work Service' or STO) that provided forced labour for Germany. To avoid capture and deportation to Germany, these bands became increasingly organized into active resistance groups.

Pétain

Philippe Pétain was a former general who was appointed marshal of France at the end of World War I. With the imminent fall of France in June 1940 in World War II, Pétain was appointed prime minister of France by President Lebrun at Bordeaux. His cabinet resolved to make peace with Germany. The entire government subsequently moved briefly to Clermont-Ferrand, then to the spa town of Vichy in central France. His government voted to transform the discredited French Third Republic into the French State, an authoritarian regime aligned with Germany.

After the war, Pétain was tried and convicted for treason. He was originally sentenced to death, but due to his age and distinguished World War I service, his sentence was commuted to life in prison. He died in 1951.

Ponot

An inhabitant of Le Puy-en-Velay, the departmental capital of the Haute-Loire. The name is thought to be derived from podium, the Latin name for *puy*, via *podot*.

Sans permis
A motor vehicle of limited size and and performance such that its driver is not required to hold a driving licence. This group of vehicles includes 'mini cars' and more recently, quadricycles. In Europe, the driver of a *sans permis* must be aged 14 years or older. The *sans permis* referred to in the poem was a very small car.

Suc
A local term, topographic rather than geological, to describe the type of steep-sided, dome-shaped hill found in large numbers in parts of the Haute-Loire, particularly in the east, but nowhere else in Europe. Those in the area around the town of Yssingeaux represent igneous extrusions of trachyphonolitic rock. In 1999, nine contiguous communes formed themselves into the Communauté de Communes des Sucs. This includes Yssingeaux and Araules, which is also mentioned in the poem.

Vichy
A town in the Auvergne department of Allier, which was the seat of the government of the French State (1940–1944) headed by Marshal Pétain. This administration, widely referred to as 'Vichy France' extended over a large part of eastern and southern France (the so-called free zone—*zone libre*), the rest of the country being under German military occupation. However, towards the end of 1942, this zone also became occupied.

Yad Vashem
The World Holocaust Remembrance Center, Israel's official memorial to the victims of the Holocaust. It is dedicated to preserving the memory of the dead, honouring Jews who fought against their Nazi oppressors and gentiles who selflessly aided Jews in need, and researching the phenomenon of the Holocaust in particular and genocide in general, with the aim of avoiding such events in the future.

TRANSLATIONS

Attention!—il est méchant!
Watch out!—he's naughty!

Pas de loup mais toujours la peur
No wolf but always the fear